The First Five Storms

Theophilus Kwek

smith|doorstop

Published 2017 by
smith|doorstop books
The Poetry Business
Bank Street Arts
32-40 Bank Street
Sheffield S1 2DS

ISBN 978-1-910367-72-8
Typeset by Utter
Printed by Biddles

smith|doorstop books are a member of Inpress:
www.inpressbooks.co.uk. Distributed by Central Books Ltd.,
99 Wallis Road, London E9 5LN

The Poetry Business gratefully acknowledges the support
of Arts Council England.

Contents

First Snow

From a window. Last night's fall in fresh veins
fills the wrinkled earth, tracks without trains,

a fifth hedge across the square fields. Light sown
as haw, thawed streams like cracks in the bone.

Beneath the treeline a fisherman's cord
corrals the low hills, spills poured silver

into seams, braided wood. Its frayed edges
spread earthward, soft chalk, the smell of sage.

Doors fling open at each scheduled station.
What begins as draught – a waiting engine

steeped in frost, footsteps quickening
along a platform's length – stirs the cabin

to praise, or something like praise: a ratchet
in the heart, cold felt as joy, for cloth

which covers the wounded scarp, the hurtling thrush,
spent farms. That through a window comes

like a thief to bless a driver's plainsong,
men in their warmed cars. The right and the wronged.

The Weaver

In late May we find the weaver's nest
unharmed, lifted up to heaven
from our hardwood floor by the laundry wires.
We watch from a room. How each day's increase
adds to that growing world some sense
of time, a loom's precise design,
choice threads, a parent's full recompense
won by the light of an evening's fire.

Within a month the chicks are hatched,
turn clamorous, feed with long beaks.
We become used to their house of thatch,
loud voices, the way she comes in flying low
as if suspended, or treading air
heavy with gift: a mantis clasped in prayer
and twine, a morning's hard hunting.
Nothing prepares us for the mystery.

How creatures love and, like us, try
to bind the ones they love. I think again
of that first January's encircling cold,
the boy with the hat his mother made,
dark wool wound tight, a woven thing.
The night he leaves without it from *The Crown*
it is a full hour before he names his loss,
walks adrift along the city's fault,

sits, comes undone. Three days
till he buys another, which weighs different
though the fabric is the same. Later he learns
it is a matter of technique, doubling
the lines for consistency, the cinch of yarn,
but believes there must be something to do
with the weeks each takes for completion,
those sprigs in the string, time's ingredient.

Road Cutting at Glanmire

'Gleann Maghair': the valley of ploughed land

They learned the hard way to a city's heart
was to drive a road into the mountain
like a river, lost between its own dry banks

with gravelled walls holding the earth in place
and fast-growing trees for the wet topsoil.
A bypass. When it was finished they came

to see the cut that had been named after them,
mounting the ridge above its strange traffic
while their own valley of ploughed land rose

a stone's throw behind the black backbone
of the new highway. Far as I could tell
from the bus window, these days the village

has a changed air, full of primary schools
and real estate. We passed a lovely church
near the auctioneer's, but without stopping

went on into Cork, taking the road which,
we were told, had been built at great cost
to shorten the journey into the city.

Fibonacci

It must have been around this time of year.
Weathered sheep, white sky, a frozen sun,
snow-hares still flecked with autumn colours,
kites flown from draughty nests. Foxes, long
gone into hiding, let alone by the royal dogs
asleep in Pisa's kennels. Nothing left to ruin
his famous experiment, not the thought
of Geronimo curled in his father's things
through warm Mediterranean nights,
dream-fingers closed on a noiseless toy
made from the tree outside, nor the sense
he finds hard to explain, waking at first light
to a quiet house, of something out of joint,
a pattern unstuck. In the end

what is it that makes him count the pairs?
One afternoon, a sign of nature's genius,
a willow-branch stealing unawares
through the window, stalks of angel's tears
frosted over in their plain geometry?
Or, at forty-seven, the inscrutable
timed tremble in the blood, age's alchemy,
which after a spell turns lead into silver,
then some lighter element? In the mean,
it's said, many seek that constant proof
to which all things must tend, and chance
upon what he alone among them gleans.
Nothing so infinite as to count as truth,
only return, which is a form of consequence.

Requiem
Grandfather, 1936-2015.

You met us again in the outer room.
White bone in miniature, glazed earth
parting the skull's cracked continents.

With love's red cloth covering the bowl,
we lined up one by one to send you home.
A pair of hands took each broken part

and joined it with the others in the pile
so the pieces belonged as they were laid,
sternum, tibia, pelvis, patella

nook to nook, against the plain design.
In cupped fingers we scooped the fire-
tempered sand, a cloud of chalk

over the precious hill. You said nothing,
content that we should have our ways of loss,
our sifted, falling silences, the plunge

of numbed hands under frigid water.
Teach me now to love, at their frayed ends
the left-behind, their washed and ashen fingers.

What Follows

Deer cull, Wytham Woods, 7th February 2015

A moment's pause before a flight of swallows
spooks the sky above the nearest trees.
Something shakes the fence-bound rows,
bursts through bracken, reappears

on fallow earth: two deer, mud-sprayed
and plunged with melt, lips puckering
to a laboured bark, dark eyes like slate
glazed in the run. My finger

leaves the shutter for long enough
that bounding across seed-rows they are gone,
the cracked frost making an ashen path
to a gap in the horse-wire thorn,

the next field, and the one beyond
where white tails vanish into wheat.
I look more closely at the ground.
Here they stood, and saw, and blinked back death

then turned with gunshot simplicity,
fled, like any creature would,
but struck on the flint of that eternity
more alive than in the burnished wood.

The Passenger

'In the months after the tsunami, taxi drivers in the coastal town of Ishinomaki reported picking up ghost passengers who asked to be brought to their destination and then disappeared, leaving their fare unpaid.' – Inquisitor, 4 February 2016

This, then, is the afterlife. A bend, a
shout, a breath of diesel, morning's murmur

staining the kerb a shade of persimmon.
A solitary confinement. No-one

else in line, birds passing like vehicles
and this way from Sendai, Charon's vessel

an old Corolla pulling up close. In
our stories, the dead follow the whirlwind

of a river's course underground, until
it comes up for air. The earth is a bell

that trembles only with water's voice
or when struck with an unnatural force,

as when Izanami drew a fire from
his whalebone comb, and saw in the loam

his beloved, Izanagi, asleep
at the foot of the well. How the god wept,

afraid! Then turned, and, bashful of his fear,
sealed death's throat with a stone. So here we are

without refuge. Out from the silent town
to the highway's shoulder, fog-lights, the sound

of brakes, front tyres arresting earth, chassis,
an open window. Lock, both doors. Release.

Magdalene

For days afterwards late Spring took its course.
A north wind came through the window-slats
and plovers returned to walk on water.
In the shorter shadows the city's groves
filled out with leaves, promised black olives
as clouds wept and bowed over the temple.
We broke bread on the roof. Said fumbling prayers
to keep the hours, returned to usual squares,
gathered each evening in our knit circles.
It was all we could do to live, despite
the wanting the waiting or the altered light
of that once-opened sky, blue as a miracle.
In time we grew acquainted with the weight
of wonder, thought less of the mystery of things,
thought them more believable. Some went back
to Galilee. Others made for other seas,
nets and fresh tackle. I watched them leave,
then stood alone in the tug of wild hyssop
at the city's sleeve, strong as love or the facts
of being known: brief night. The lightness of stone.

24.6.16

*Red kites, native to Turkey, Morocco, and parts of Europe, were declared 'vermin'
by the English crown and hunted nearly to extinction. They were successfully
reintroduced to the UK in 1989.*

No red kites over the field this morning.
However hard I looked, I could not find

a single cresting pair, their high crosses
invisible – as if unpitched from the grass.

No dry swoop, no sounding. No clatter from
morning's fed sparrows rising in alarm,

no hare's carcass eaten behind our wall,
nothing astir. No courting on the fell

in curious patterns, no stumbling display
of swift shadows bending above the Wye.

No haunt. No song. Only the heaven's blue
graceless fire, and then as a ghost pursued

across a moor, the hunting-horn's burly
cry
                    crucify, crucify, crucify.

Sophia

In 1818, Sir Thomas Stamford Raffles, newlywed husband of Sophia, Governor-General of Bencoolen, surveyed the island of Singapore, which was made a British colony early the next year.

i.

12 December, 1818.
Governor-General's Residence, Bencoolen.

Last night, my love, I took the nameless book
that arrived with our mail on Thursday's ship
and sat down to read. In that shapely dark
one by one the servants kept their hours,
leaving the gate unlocked (as you prefer)
as they crept downhill to their inventions.
Nothing moved, but on the forest's lip
something glimmered with a sailor's patience:

a slip of sand, a turning in the shallows,
an unmade sea scuffing the glass surface
with its swallowed things. I thought of you,
the men in their tossing berths, the night's
empty heat, and beyond the shoal of islands
a breath of earth, void, then the firmament.

ii.

12 December, 1858.
Highwood House, Mill Hill, London.

This remains sharpest in my memory:
the day you went walking into the wind
from a corner of that special island
so spectral now, yet with its harbour, then
the pearl of our possessions. How we made
our livings there, rejoicing as we found
a world so large, and of our own devising,
that you longed to know it, end to end.

As the light fell short you came back trembling,
stood bareheaded in the dousing rain, yelled
for a mirror. Told how even the men
had fled when they saw you approaching, pale
arms outstretched in a token of friendship.
I held on to your hands and let you weep.

Occurrence

Thames Valley Police, No. 43150331197, 6.35 p.m. on 23ʳᵈ November, 2015:
the victim was struck on the face with a metal rod by men in an unidentified car,
on Oriel Square, breaking his glasses. No assailant could be traced.

Nothing much then, now nearly unseen –
a cut beneath the eye. A bruise, fading
to skin, frown and furrow, fine print. How

soon the body grieves, forgives how easily
it gives. Already these marks are marks
of other things. Sleepless lines that mar

an early frost. Fields turned for planting,
sandstone shorn against the river's brink.
A fishhook's incline, the doubling pitch

of flight like a whaler's reckoning. In
the hollow of a bridge the water leaves
no scar, only trembling. A sound gone

as if from a whipped bowstring, between
where the arrow flies and, at each end,
thread spliced so as to pucker wood: the eyes.

The Crossing

'When any of the fugitives said, "Let me go over", the men of Gilead said to him ..."Say Shibboleth," and he said, "Sibboleth," for he could not pronounce it right. Then they seized him and slaughtered him at the fords of the Jordan, [and thus] 42,000 of the Ephraimites fell.' – Judges 12:5-6

Calf-deep in water and no turning back,
we bury our swords in sacks of grain,
smear on wet loam to make our faces dark.

Black hours. The riverbed clings to our skin
as we plan our way home across the marsh
to where a firm shape of the land begins:

Tribesmen, with our heavy gear and horses,
bringing a full harvest. The first sentries
take us at our word, and, lifting a measure

of dry corn from our bags, wish us peace.
In the pale light we haul the animals
champing at their ropes into the morass,

trust our luck and the still-distant swell
with our feet, eyes. Then from too close
among our submerged ranks, a yell –

A bucking horse, a rock, rope loosed
from the grip – that makes the watchmen turn,
curse, fix us with a sterner glare. Years

later on Jordan's bank another man
will comfort his people, *by your words
you will be justified.* Here on the open

water there is nothing, nothing to hold
as the word comes faltering to our lips,
wide nothing that makes our voices heard

above the river's lisp, nothing like sleep
or the comfort of sleep. As we speak
the mud slips off our faces into the deep.

Blue

Years later, I saw in the Ashmolean
precious plates, fine porcelain

of the best handiwork, that stood
down the aisle on the first floor

in their blue cases. Some of them by then
I already knew by heart, having gone

to school in the refurbished building
where we painted, one year, a semblance

of a low Victorian house that sat out of reach
as our bus-route narrowed to a bridge.

Others I had never seen, but were the twins
of a bright, winding city where I spent

hours salvaged from school and home
with my own widening strides marking time,

close likenesses copied onto each gleaming
dish from Calcutta and Penang.

Behind Grandmother's house there was once
a factory where, in her motley tongue,

she told me they used to blow blue glass
for windowpanes, wine-bottles, flasks.

I pressed my hands to the cabinet
full of china, and dreamt that I could touch

the tea services, with their beautiful necks
too thin, too tall for proper use.

Dead Man's Savings Won't Go To Wife

*'Ms Diao, a Chinese national ... claimed to love Mr Soon and to meet him for
dinner about once a week, but could not say why she loved him, and claimed
they would eat fish, when Mr Soon did not.'*
    – The Straits Times, 8th September 2016

How could I explain? *Your first glance*
was that of an old lover's. All guilt,
no charm. As I washed the breakfast things
you struggled with your shirt, belt,

Looked away when I knelt
to lace your shoes. Those mornings
turned out to be my favourite –
us two in the park downstairs,

Your arm on mine as joggers passed,
wings touching as we flew. Months
wore on. You ate little, spoke less,
but still I knew you'd *give a thousand coins*

for my smile, the way you'd sit
by the door waiting, or press a little extra
into my palm as I went to market
for threadfin or garoupa,

something for myself. For you this
was enough, an extravagance, nearly,
of joy. And I? *I loved the house*
And the crows that nested there,

the missed appointments, separate beds,
how you always left the radio on.
In the end, they said,
you gave no last instructions,

so it wasn't clear my claim was genuine.
That, I tried not to mind.
I wish you'd told them how much this would mean.
One who knows my voice is hard to find.

* Italics denote loose translations of Chinese idioms for love:
一见如故, 比翼双飞, 千金买笑, 爱屋及乌, 知音难觅.

23

Loch na Fuaiche

from Cong, 25 minutes via R345 and R300.

No telling on this drive, what must
take years to know: how love is found

in a valley delta, where two fields meet
in stone – a low wall, raised here by hand

from the slow gathering on either side
of rock, large enough to unearth a crop

or throw a plough sideways. A difficult task
given how, from near the mountaintop

each spring, loosed in its thaw,
the river brings new boulders toward the sea

and leaves them by the weir. Or even how
faintly the loch wears the county's edge

till fields are sunk, and disappear
with a season's planting, all their names

and boundaries intact. Every now and then
a winter still comes to fill the glen

so all we can see is the black backbone
of our stones underwater, no more a wall

but a path, flood-lit in the shallow depths,
that links the far sides of the loch, and then

rises, to join hands with the lifting land.

The First Five Storms

Beginning November 2015, when the UK Meteorological Office began to name its storms.

i. Abigail

We sat up late one night to watch the sky
knowing where they slept, still, in their fury,

a den of them curled on the red-rimmed ledge
of tomorrow's weather. As we talked, we kept

our predictions close: how long
before the year's, and our own winters would align,

or the rest of our days reach in to join fingers
with the season's slow dusk, and disappear.

What came afterwards, or perhaps who,
surprised us both. It was as if they knew

something we didn't about earth's velocity,
the speed of spring, time's machine. Soon the first

trains arrived at King's Cross with Berwick's rain.
It was then that we learnt to give them names.

ii. Barney

Here we sensed the war and tremble of it,
the fallen scaffolding, the leaf-filled storm,
in land-bound Oxford a river's solvent march.
For all of what we knew as Christmas
it came unspent, and there was not a room
that did not seal itself against that tide
of fog and rain, a rippling in the sky

Like the wake of a wake. When it was past
we looked out, and went back into the street
where there was death, and ice, and such a calm
of winter, road-pressed tracks, a dark *bonsai*
stooped by a window of our chimneyed home.
We stood, then went in our cars to church,
and scraped our shoes, and left the dog outside.

iii. Clodagh

We made the landing that we thought we would
three hours late, and below the flush deck
where drivers sat at their cards, stretched and stood
the worse for wear. You had slept through the thick
of it, so didn't feel the sudden fall
as our hull found Dublin's sterner quay, and lodged
shuddering against the sea's dredged wall.
above the harbour, a glassy-dark ridge –

horizontal, like the sea's calmed veneer –
stood across from where a guileless city lay
behind a crowd of windows. I had come here
to make resolutions, taste the grey
Christmas skies you loved, but found instead
fine rain, and land underfoot; gold and myrrh.

iv. Desmond

When you had gone up to bed, that night,
a wind came and touched a corner of the roof
which sang, through the shingles that had come loose
and shook the nest, which had been built inside.
How late, the storm that followed close behind
locked in all its pent determination
that even love's sentry was, briefly, then,
asleep, her once watchful head dipped within.

She made no sound as, like a ship astern,
her bower was rushed by the northern rain.
This morning I saw her young: unlearned,
alive. I cannot explain, love, but I knew
how different they seemed, and how they sang
all the louder in the rain, and flew.

v. Eva

And after several days' lowering,
white like a dream of white, ghosting snow,
there and not there as we fled from town
one pure winter's morning. Wanting to make
the most of daylight, we set out early
and with the first glare came up to the track,
full-bodied, the scent of January's mowing
fresh on fallen grass: a season's dowry,

made in our time as the meadow hankered
under a cloth of cold. What could ever come
of such small beginnings? Already the frost
was melting on the path, which, unbroken,
would put dry earth to grass, and then in time
turn road to wood, and sky, and bark, and moss.

Notes

'First Snow' and 'Magdalene' were part of a suite which won the Jane Martin Prize for Poetry in 2015, and 'Magdalene' was also placed second in The Oxonian Review Poetry Competition in that year. 'Occurrence' was part of a suite placed second in *The Adroit Journal*'s Poetry Prize in 2016, and 'What Follows' was placed third in *The London Magazine*'s Poetry Prize in 2015. 'The Weaver' was commended in the Four Corners Poetry Competition in 2015, 'Loch Na Fuaiche' was highly commended in the Gregory O'Donoghue International Poetry Competition in 2015, and 'The Passenger' was shortlisted for the Basil Bunting Poetry Prize in 2016.

'First Snow' and 'The Weaver' were first published in *Giving Ground* (Singapore: Ethos Books, 2016). They appear here by kind permission of the publishers – and with many thanks for their enduring support. Thanks are also due to the editors of the following publications where some of these poems previously appeared: *Antiphon, Coldnoon, Eastlit, Irish Examiner, Irish Literary Review, Kingdom Poets, The Honest Ulsterman, The Interpreter's House, The London Magazine, The Lonely Crowd, The Mays XXIV, The Missing Slate, Southword,* and *THINK Journal.*